SKATE THE WORLD

SKATE THE WORLD

Photographing One World of Skateboarding

JONATHAN MEHRING

FOREWORD BY TONY HAWK

NATIONAL GEOGRAPHIC

WASHINGTON, D.C.

This book is dedicated to skateboarders everywhere, for exercising the freedom to interpret the world in your own way, for believing in yourself, and for following your own path. —JM

A youth headstands on a skateboard —Birmingham, Alabama.

JERRY HSU ~ BUENOS AIRES, ARGENTINA
Trick: 180 nosegrind *(p. 2)*

AARON "JAWS" HOMOKI ~ UTAH, U.S.A.
Trick: Kickflip *(pp. 4-5)*

JOEY PEPPER, DAVID GRAVETTE, JOSH MATTHEWS, MARIUS SYVANEN, AND RAME TCHACK ~ LA PAZ, BOLIVIA
Trick: Hill bombing *(pp. 6-7)*

MATT BERGER ~ ADDIS ABABA, ETHIOPIA
Trick: 5-0 grind *(pp. 8-9)*

AL PARTANEN ~ BANGALORE, INDIA
Trick: Backside boneless *(pp. 10-11)*

JAMIE THOMAS ~ KABUL, AFGHANISTAN
Trick: Tank ollie *(pp. 12-13)*

KEVIN "SPANKY" LONG AND JERRY HSU ~ ISTANBUL, TURKEY *(pp. 14-15)*

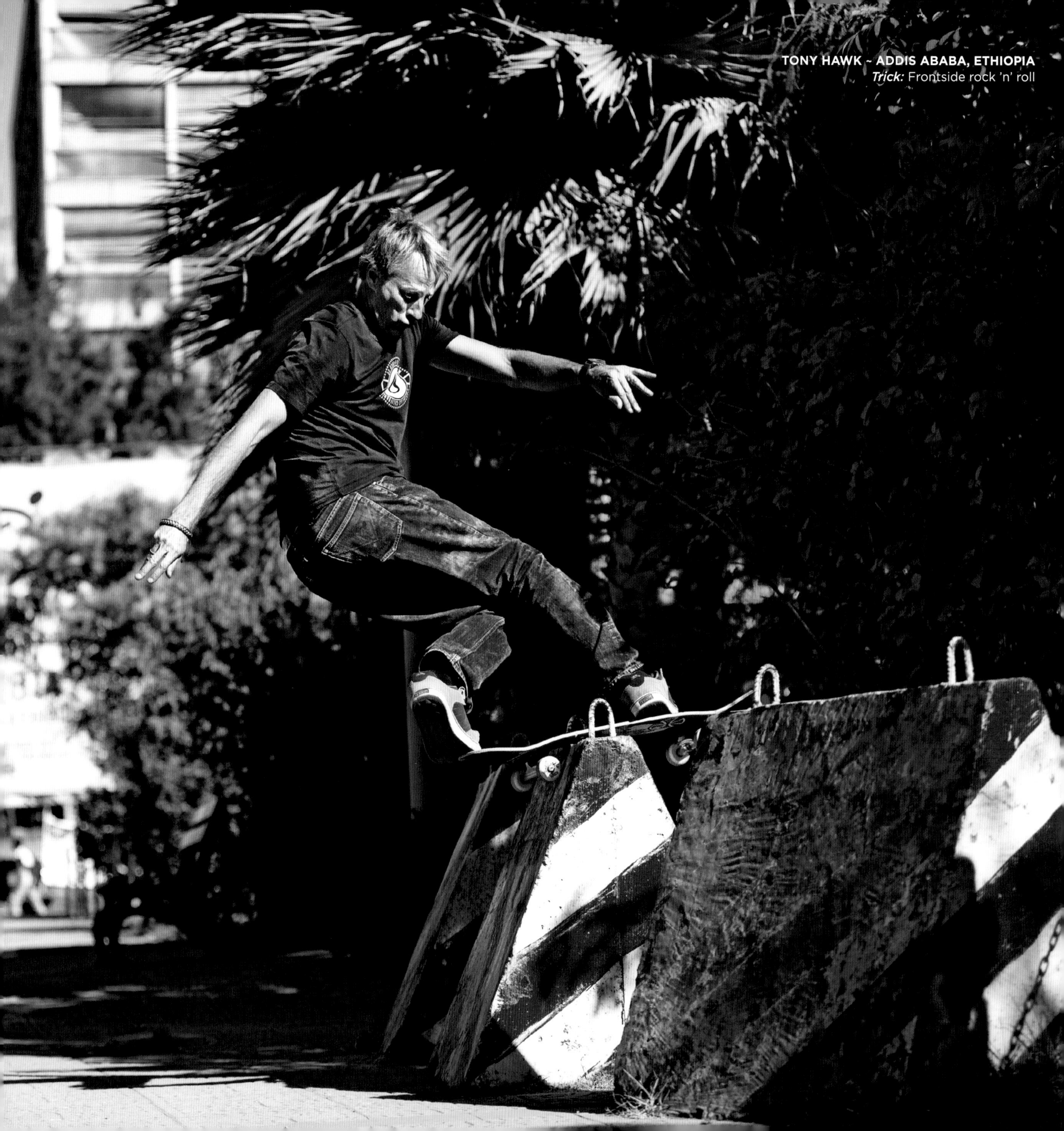

TONY HAWK ~ ADDIS ABABA, ETHIOPIA
Trick: Frontside rock 'n' roll

FOREWORD TONY HAWK

When I first stepped onto a skateboard at age nine, the world seemed impossibly big and entirely devoid of other skateboarders. But all I needed were a few friends who shared my interest and the nearby skatepark, which became our sanctuary. It hadn't even occurred to me that anyone outside southern California cared about skateboarding, and I never imagined that it could become a legitimate career.

As skateboarding grew in popularity throughout the 1980s, small scenes began to take hold internationally. Once I became a pro, I traveled to Japan, Australia, Brazil, Europe, and South Africa and discovered that skateboarding had become a great equalizer. It brought together people from varying socioeconomic backgrounds. The sport even bridged language barriers—we all spoke the same slang! I loved seeing the fanaticism of foreign skaters when I'd show up to perform. In broken English, they'd call out specific tricks, and I'd do my best to oblige them.

Skateboarding waned in popularity in the early 1990s, but thanks to the spread of video games and televised competitions like the X Games, it experienced a comeback in the 2000s that was bigger than anyone could have predicted.

I am proud to have been one of the sport's ambassadors abroad. In the past decade, I've performed in such unlikely places as India, Argentina, West Africa, Chile, Poland, Russia, and Ethiopia, where I had the pleasure of working with Jonathan Mehring and other skaters to build the first concrete half-pipe in the city of Addis Ababa.

In the age of YouTube and social media, skateboarding has become more global and more accessible than ever before. The allure is undeniable—immediate gratification, daredevil antics, and artistic flair. But more important, as skaters advance from tic-tacs to ollies to kickflips to crooked grinds on 20-stair rails, and even to 20-foot aerials, they learn a lesson that will serve them through life: Perseverance pays.

I have no doubt that skateboarding will continue to expand internationally, and I'm fairly certain that it will become an Olympic sport. I look forward to watching the sport that I fell in love with as a nine-year-old continue to grow in unlikely places and continue to transcend race, religion, language, and economic barriers—and maybe make the world a little smaller along the way. ∎

INTRODUCTION JONATHAN MEHRING

Commonly called a sport, skateboarding is actually a form of self-expression akin to dance or painting. A skater learns tricks and applies them to found obstacles called "spots"—the slanted facade of a building, a ledge, a handrail, stairs, marble plazas, loading ramps, cellar doors, curbs, or any kind of urban structure with a decent amount of space and smooth ground. The board is the artist's paintbrush, and the world is his or her canvas.

My first spot was a homemade ramp that an elementary school friend and I cobbled together from plywood and piles of firewood. Mostly we just rode back and forth, but the experience was exhilarating. By the time I was in high school, I was skating with friends in my hometown of Charlottesville, Virginia, and taking road trips to Washington, D.C., just two hours away, where endless pavement and granite and marble plazas called to us. Skating became my identity. It was a social scene, an adrenaline fueled activity, and a way of life. Society was less accepting of skateboarding then, which, to my rebellious teenage mind, made the sport even more intoxicating. I was hooked.

I discovered photography in high school, and it seemed to go hand in hand with skateboarding. I became obsessed with skate magazines, the photographers, and their techniques. I carried this passion with me through art school, and was crazy and naive enough to think that I could turn my two passions into a career. And, somehow, it worked!

Slap Skateboard Magazine sent me on my first tour, during which I photographed top professional skaters in Hong Kong. I remember getting up at dawn to shoot one of my favorite photos from that first trip, which actually made it into this book (pages 174-75). After a few years of shooting on assignment, I grew restless. I wanted to capture the adventuresome spirit of skating in my photography and to seek out new locations around the globe that had rarely, if ever, been skated.

I wasn't exactly sure what I was looking for until I organized a 2007 trip from Moscow to Beijing along the Trans-Siberian Railway. During the two-month odyssey, a group of pro skaters and I visited cities across Russia, Mongolia, and China. Each town had its own waxed curb, small skatepark, or dilapidated ramp behind a building. We were on the opposite side of the

Earth, and we met skaters just like us at every stop. We spoke different languages and came from different cultures, but skateboarding became our shared language—a sort of subculture in and of itself. This was the connection I had been searching for.

Skateboarders share the understanding that we've suffered for the same cause. We've conquered our fears, hit the pavement hard, seen our own blood, gotten up, and tried again. Skaters have an intense inner drive to seek out challenges and master them. We do not give up easily. It's that restless heart of skating that captivates me and keeps me coming back for more—the excitement, the danger, and the glory of landing a trick after hours of failed attempts, and the freedom it all represents.

And it was this restless heart that drew me to India in 2013. I became acquainted with the good work the Levi's company was doing in India with the Holystoked Collective. The company funded a new skatepark for the youths of Bangalore and taught the locals how to mix and pour concrete to make ramps themselves. Kids had a place to play, and the locals learned the skills to keep skating alive in their own communities. Throughout this book, I've spotlighted the extraordinary efforts of the international skate community to help kids in need, including ongoing projects led by the Levi's Skateboarding brand, which has generously sponsored this book.

While I've covered skate scenes around the world, there are still many places that I haven't been to yet. So I invited some of my colleagues to be a part of this book. These top skateboard photographers from around the globe have generously provided images of places and skaters that I haven't yet shot and that needed a presence here.

Most of the skaters featured in this book are professionals whom I've had the honor of photographing. But I've also tried to capture the local skate scenes I've encountered in my travels and many of the kids and characters I've met along the way.

What I hope comes across in this book is that skateboarding is a positive force in our world. It's a challenging activity that captivates its participants at an early age and guides them during their formative years and beyond. It provides a sense of community to otherwise disenfranchised youths who may not enjoy more popular team sports. It accepts those who don't fit in elsewhere and gives them confidence and purpose. Skateboarding is more than a form of entertainment. It's a lifestyle that transcends social, economic, and cultural barriers around the globe. ▪

CHAPTER 1

NORTH

AMERICA

TOY MACHINE SKATE TEAM ~ BIRMINGHAM, ALABAMA

"SKATEBOARDING BRINGS YOU FREEDOM. FREEDOM FROM GROWING UP, FREEDOM FROM RESPONSIBILITY, FREEDOM FROM REALITY."

—LEO ROMERO, PROFESSIONAL SKATEBOARDER

t was the year 2000, and I'd just graduated from college. Two friends and I packed up my dilapidated 1984 Toyota Camry and hit the road for a month. We headed out from Richmond, Virginia, and circled the continental United States, looking for skate spots in each city along the way. We could afford gas, food, and a campground each night for almost the whole trip. We were just a few hundred dollars short, but we'd cross that bridge when we came to it. And we knew we had skating on our side. Inevitably, we met other skaters who let us crash on their couches, fed us, and looked out for us when we needed help.

That was the beginning of my travels with skateboard in hand and the trip that helped lead me to my current home. I checked out the skate scene in many cities that summer, but I'd always had my eye on New York City. It has an allure, a style, and I knew that my photography would thrive there. Los Angeles was, and is, the world hub for skating, but the sunny skies and smooth pavement of California didn't inspire me the way the unique colors and textures of New York did. New York can be frustrating for skaters because of its old, rough pavement, but it also rewards persistence.

New York is one of the most challenging places to shoot. My photo shoot with pro skater Dylan Rieder in Manhattan (pages 44-45) was a case in point. I was balancing on top of a fire hydrant to get my vantage point, while Dylan tried not to lose his board, which would surely send it careening into traffic. Pedestrians walked through my frame, cars zoomed by mid-shot, rocky pavement threatened to jam Dylan's wheels. But it was totally worth it. It's well known among skaters and photographers that if you can get a trick on film in New York City, it's probably going to look amazing.

As in other places around the country, skateboarding in New York has slowly become more accepted by society. Since the sport first became popular in the 1960s, a lot of people viewed skateboarders as rebellious hell-raisers. But that image is fading fast. In California schools, skateboarding is now a gym class activity. So many skaters cruise down the streets of Los Angeles and San Francisco that it feels as if the cities themselves live and breathe skateboarding. And skateparks abound in nearly every American city and in smaller towns.

The popularity of the sport has spread throughout North America. On Go Skateboarding Day 2014, more than 10,000 skaters pushed through downtown Mexico City in celebration of their pursuit. And Canada has seen a progression of skate culture similar to that in the United States, with main hubs in Vancouver, Toronto, and Montreal.

Much to the dismay of many skateboarders, the sport is becoming more mainstream. But that's the great thing about skateboarding. Our tight-knit community grows stronger with every new skater who comes along. ▨

VAN WASTELL ~ RALEIGH, NORTH CAROLINA, U.S.A.
Trick: Full pipe transfer

DANNY WAY ~ AGUANGA, CALIFORNIA, U.S.A.
Trick: World-record-setting 23-foot method air

JOSH KALIS ~ PHILADELPHIA, PENNSYLVANIA, U.S.A.
Trick: Switch crooked grind

"THIS PHOTO SUMS UP MY TIME IN NEW YORK CITY: WEATHER-BEATEN, BLACK-AND-WHITE, OUT OF FOCUS, EXCITING, AND DANGEROUS."

—ANDREW PETERS, PHOTOGRAPHER

BRIAN DELATORRE ~ NEW YORK CITY, U.S.A.
Trick: Frontside ollie

SKATEBOARDERS RALLY AT THE "BACK TO THE BANKS" CONTEST AT THE BROOKLYN BANKS, A FAMOUS SKATE SPOT UNDER THE BROOKLYN BRIDGE – NEW YORK CITY, U.S.A.

"SKATING BRINGS YOUR MIND AND BODY TO A PLACE OF SERIOUS DETERMINATION, NO MATTER THE PAIN YOU SUFFER TO RIDE AWAY."

—BRANDON WESTGATE

BRANDON WESTGATE ~ EL PASO, TEXAS, U.S.A.
Trick: 360 flip

40

LIZZIE ARMANTO ~ MOORPARK, CALIFORNIA, U.S.A.
Trick: Layback smith grind

RICK HOWARD ~ TORONTO, ONTARIO, CANADA
Trick: Bluntslide

"SKATEBOARDING IS AN INDIVIDUAL ACTIVITY, BUT WITHOUT A CREW OF LIKE-MINDED FRIENDS IT WOULDN'T BE THE SAME."

—JONATHAN MEHRING

A GROUP OF FRIENDS CALLED THE SUGAR GANG ~ BRONX, NEW YORK, U.S.A.

DYLAN RIEDER ~ NEW YORK CITY, U.S.A.
Trick: Backside smith grind to backside tailslide

46

TYSHAWN JONES ~ NEW YORK CITY, U.S.A.
Trick: Skitching a ride

"I MISSED A SIMILAR PHOTO OF THIS AMAZING TRICK IN 2007, BUT I WAS LUCKY TO HAVE IT REPEAT ITSELF YEARS LATER."

—ATIBA JEFFERSON, PHOTOGRAPHER

ANDREW REYNOLDS ~ VANCOUVER, BRITISH COLUMBIA, CANADA
Trick: Frontside kickflip

A BUSINESSMAN EYES SKATEBOARDERS AND A MOBILE
SKATE SHOP ~ ASTOR PLACE, NEW YORK CITY, U.S.A.

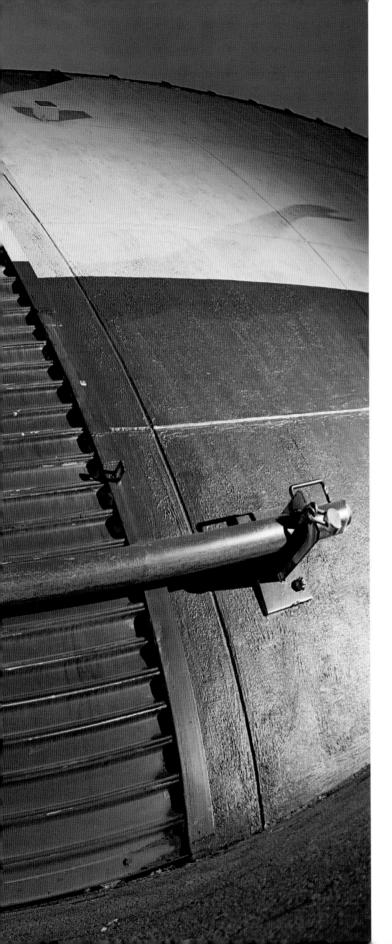

"THERE MUST BE A THOUSAND ROLL-DOWN GATES WITH BARS IN FRONT OF 'EM IN BROOKLYN. MOST AREN'T KNOWN SPOTS, THEY ARE JUST THERE. I LIKE THAT ASPECT."

—JASON DILL

JASON DILL ~ BROOKLYN, NEW YORK, U.S.A.
Trick: Backside 5-0 grind

ALEX OLSON ~ NEW YORK CITY, U.S.A.
Trick: Wallride

DAKOTA SERVOLD AND AARON "JAWS" HOMOKI ~ BOISE, IDAHO, U.S.A.
Trick: Fakie air and backside air doubles

JOSH KALIS PUSHES ACROSS THE SAN FRANCISCO–OAKLAND
BAY BRIDGE ~ SAN FRANCISCO, CALIFORNIA, U.S.A.

WOUNDED KNEE
Pine Ridge, South Dakota, U.S.A.

Twelve-year-old Peyton was dead center and leading the way down a steep hill, full commitment and determination in his eyes. Three-quarters of the way down, kids behind him started bailing into the grass, skateboards skidding out from under them. Peyton looked back to see what was happening, and it was all over. His focus gone, he lost control, and it only took a couple of overcompensated turns to send him flying. Fighting back tears, he regained his composure as we walked back toward Wounded Knee 4-Directions Skatepark, where he and his friends spent most of their time.

Everyone who skates for any length of time has had the experience of "bombing" that first hill, and inevitably everyone will "slam" hard at some point. And then you get up and try again. It could be called an involuntary initiation to skateboarding—and perhaps to real life.

When Pearl Jam bass player and avid skateboarder Jeff Ament and the Vitalogy Foundation funded the building of this skatepark on South Dakota's Pine Ridge Indian Reservation, he understood the sport's power to change kids' lives. Pine Ridge, home to tens of thousands of Oglala Lakota Indians, wasn't all that different from his hometown in rural Montana. Isolation and alcoholism had taken a toll on both communities.

(Kids at Wounded Knee 4-Directions Skatepark, top to bottom) Emily Autumn Earring performs a frontside 5-0 grind; Darien and Wakinyan fix a board as DJ Vitalis airs out of the bowl behind them; Jake Roubideaux arrives on horseback.

"YOU HAVE TO GIVE THE YOUNGEST GENERATION HOPE.
YOU GIVE THEM AN OUTLET. I THINK BUILDING
A SKATEPARK IS THAT THING."

—JEFF AMENT

Wounded Knee 4-Directions Skatepark ~ Pine Ridge, South Dakota, U.S.A.

Skateboarding became Ament's survival, and he knew it would transform the youth population in Pine Ridge as well.

The reservation is dry, but the alcohol sold at a state-run liquor store right across the border in Nebraska has a firm grip on a large percentage of the population. In addition to the problems of alcoholism and drug abuse, the reservation is experiencing an epidemic of teen suicide. For the skaters of Pine Ridge, the park is a beacon of hope. It provides a confidence-boosting physical activity and a sense of community and belonging. It gives them a safe place to go to hone their skills and hang out with friends. Foundations like the Stronghold Society and Wounded Knee Skateboards help support the young skaters. One of the rules is that if you want to ride at Wounded Knee, you have to be sober.

The park has no security and no supervision, except for the older skaters watching over the younger ones, and it doesn't appear that it needs any. One police officer told me that there were only ten arrests during the reservation's annual powwow in 2014—down significantly from prior years—and gave much of the credit to the skatepark. The kids who might normally be misbehaving, drinking, or breaking the law had become skateboarders. In Pine Ridge, where there isn't much else to focus on, the old skate motto "Live to skate, skate to live" takes on new significance.

Skateboarders wait to take their run during a contest at Wounded Knee

MARIUS SYVANEN ~ MADRID, SPAIN
Trick: Backside kickflip

"CAN'T LET SPANISH KING JUAN CARLOS I DOWN, IT WAS A PRIVILEGE AND HONOR SKATING IN HIS PRESENCE."

—MARIUS SYVANEN

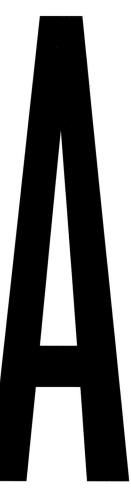**A** massive barge floated in the channel next to a shipbuilding yard. It was covered with stacks of wood that looked enticingly skateable. I had just arrived in Rotterdam, Holland, for a week-long photography contest. The photographers were instructed to handpick three professional skaters and to shoot the best skate photo we could within the city limits.

Waterfronts are often packed with colors, textures, and obstacles that make for amazing skate photos, so I took my team straight to the New Meuse River. The barge site was too good to pass up. It was essential to find a way to get on board. Somehow we persuaded the security guards to introduce us to the boss. As luck would have it, the project manager was a former skater. We were in!

His workers moved wood around on the barge with their cranes, helping us build skate spots, like the one shown on pages 80-81. The photo on pages 68-69 was shot from the roof of the crane, nearly 100 feet off the ground. I took some of my favorite photos that day.

Unfortunately, that never would have happened back home in the States. European countries tend to be more tolerant of skateboarding than the United States is. Plus, Europe's well-designed public spaces are virtual gold mines for skaters. Spanish cities are among the best of the best. Public parks, curvaceous architecture, and marble-lined streets make Barcelona a top skateboarding destination. And most important, you are allowed to skate nearly all of it.

It's hard to believe that the statue in Zaragoza, Spain, on page 78, and the transitioned wall in Gran Canaria, Spain, on page 79, were not built specifically for skateboarding.

In recent years, Copenhagen, Denmark, has taken a unique approach to urban development by building creative spaces designed for all types of sports, including skateboarding. The government has chosen to make the city skate-friendly, in contrast to many American cities, where public areas are designed to keep skateboarders away. Many basketball courts in Copenhagen are surrounded by semicircular ramps, and playgrounds have skateable obstacles at their edges (pages 94-95). In Roskilde, Denmark, architects even designed a drainage ditch as a skatepark.

In Russia and other eastern European countries with Soviet architecture, the granite and marble monuments are magnets for skateboarders. There is something about an old statue of Lenin with a perfect bank at the bottom of it that says "amazing skate spot" (pages 86-87).

Great skate locations can be old or new. The back of the Louvre Museum in Paris is a notoriously skateable spot, as is the Barcelona Museum of Contemporary Art. Skaters everywhere seek new spots and settings in which to express themselves. In Europe, anywhere you see smooth ground and unusual curves and banks, you are bound to find skaters. ▪

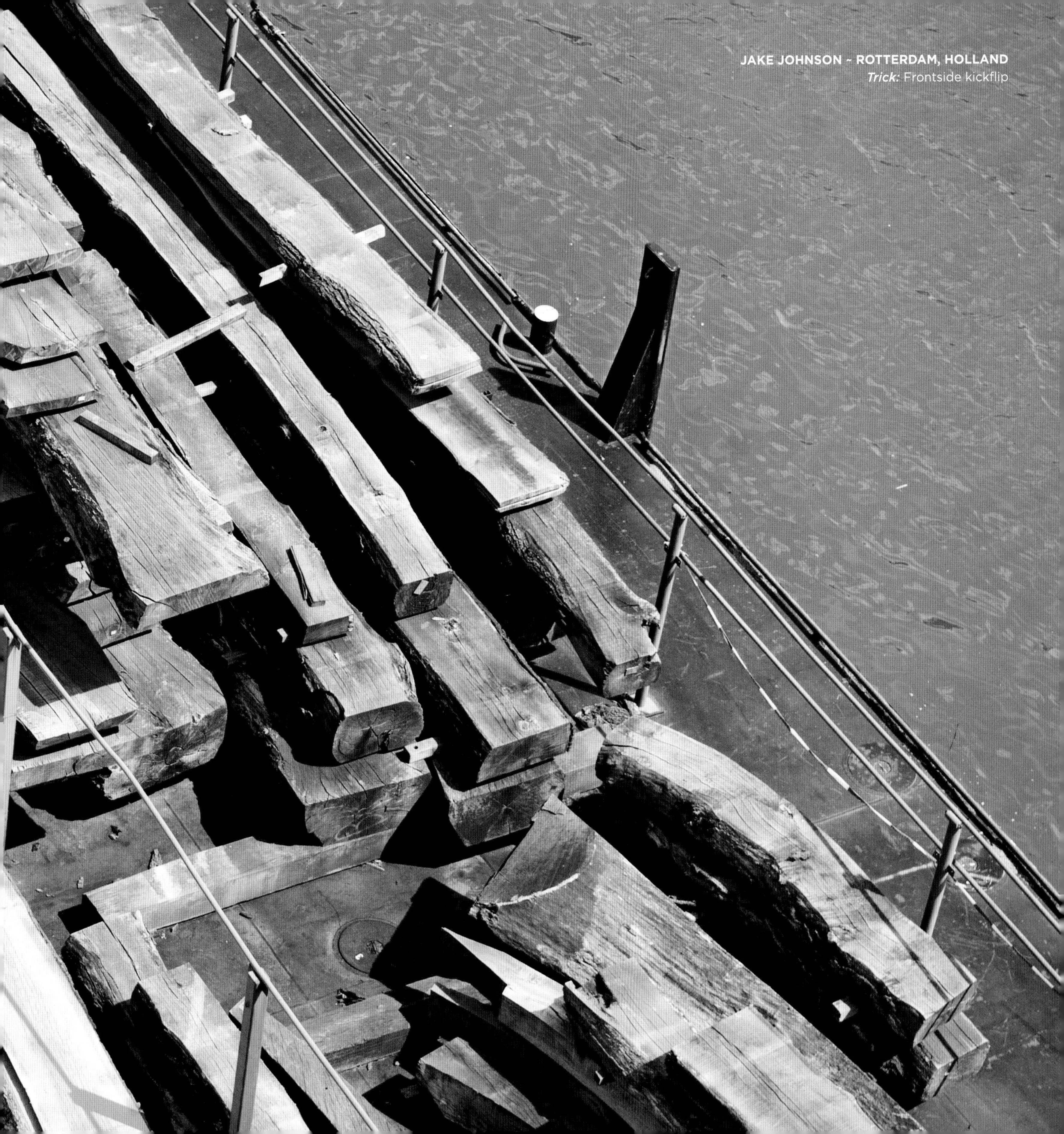

JAKE JOHNSON – ROTTERDAM, HOLLAND
Trick: Frontside kickflip

"DESPITE THE CONSTANT SWARMS OF OBLIVIOUS TOURISTS, THIS SPOT—IN SUCH AN EPIC SETTING— MADE IT TOO GOOD TO PASS UP."

—KEVIN "SPANKY" LONG

KEVIN "SPANKY" LONG ~ ISTANBUL, TURKEY
Trick: Wallie

DAN DREHOBL ~ SÈTE, FRANCE
Trick: Frontside air

TWO CHILDREN DISCOVER SKATEBOARDING ~ WARSAW, POLAND.

ADAM ALFARO ~ PARIS, FRANCE

"YOU COULD ARGUE THAT SKATING IS OVER 50 PERCENT MENTAL. CONTESTS CAN MAKE OR BREAK YOUR CONCENTRATION; SOME CHOKE WHILE OTHERS DON'T."

—JONATHAN MEHRING

JOSEF JATTA ~ COPENHAGEN, DENMARK
Trick: Stalefish

ANTHONY PAPPALARDO ~ ZARAGOZA, SPAIN
Trick: 5050 grind

**GUY MARIANO ~ GRAN CANARIA,
CANARY ISLANDS, SPAIN**
Trick: Switch crooked grind

KENNY ANDERSON ~ ROTTERDAM, HOLLAND
Trick: Backside tailslide

"IT'S AN AMAZING FEELING TO SEE HOW BIG SKATEBOARDING HAS GROWN OVER THE YEARS."

—THEOTIS BEASLEY

FANS LINE UP AT A SKATE SHOP TO GET AUTOGRAPHS
FROM PRO SKATEBOARDERS ERIC KOSTON
AND THEOTIS BEASLEY ~ BARCELONA, SPAIN.

ANTHONY PAPPALARDO ~ BARCELONA, SPAIN
Trick: Drop in 5050

KENNY REED ~ MOSCOW, RUSSIA
Trick: Noseblunt slide

"NOTHING BEATS COPENHAGEN IN THE SUMMER. IT'S A HAPPY AND FREE-SPIRITED CITY WHERE PEOPLE SOAK UP LIFE."

—AL PARTANEN

AL PARTANEN ~ COPENHAGEN, DENMARK
Trick: Frontside rock 'n' roll

MARK GONZALES AND THE KROOKED
SKATEBOARDS TEAM ~ PARIS, FRANCE

"YOU CAN'T FIND ANY BETTER POST-COLD WAR SPOT THAN PART OF A MISSILE AT AN ABANDONED MILITARY BASE."

—KIRILL KOROBKOV, JOURNALIST

VLAD ESAULKOV RIDES A DISCARDED
TRANSCONTINENTAL MISSILE ~ KHARKIV, UKRAINE.

ERIC KOSTON ~ COPENHAGEN, DENMARK
Trick: Ollie one-foot

KYLE WALKER ~ ATHENS, GREECE
Trick: Half-cab heelflip

STEPPE SIDE

Malmö, Sweden

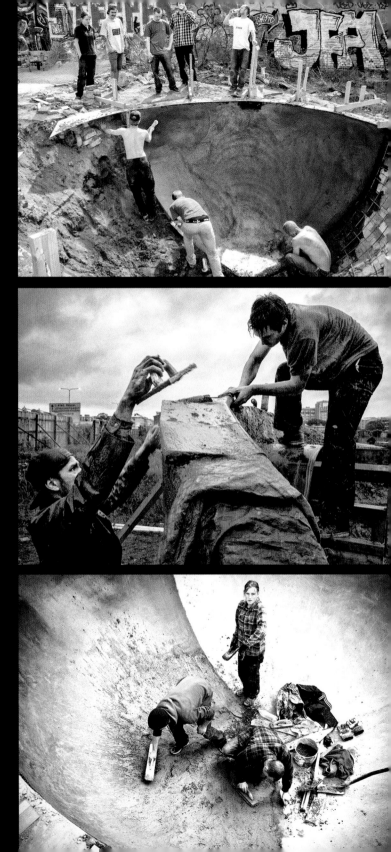

Walking down a nondescript street, I spotted the hole in a tall, wooden fence. I had heard stories about this place for years. I stepped through the hole and into a concrete paradise of graffiti-covered ramps and transitions—the infamous Steppe Side skatepark. It had a magical feel. It spoke of freedom and fun. At first glance, the ramps and transitions seemed random and awkward, but after skating for a while, I began to understand the flow of the park and how it made so many tricks possible.

To skate Steppe Side is to pay homage to the park that popularized the DIY (do-it-yourself) skatepark movement in Europe. In 2004, professional skater and Malmö resident Pontus Alv had grown tired of skating the same old spots in his hometown. He had an idea: He would gather his friends and start building a completely original skatepark—a social sculpture.

Like Alv, most skaters are inherently optimists. They have to be. Who in their right mind believes, "Yes, I can do this," when looking down the length of a huge handrail or gap, or when trying a super-technical trick on a tall ledge for weeks at a time until they can land it maybe just once? With the same abandon, Alv and his friends set off to build their park.

With a little bit of cash, a lot of concrete, and some locally sourced scrap materials, they were up and

Steppe Side under construction • Malmö, Sweden

"THE BEAUTIFUL THING WITH THE PROJECT IS NOT THE SKATING BUT GETTING TOGETHER WITH YOUR FRIENDS AND CREATING SOMETHING. THE SKATING IS A BONUS."

—PONTUS ALV

Andreas Lindstrom performs a frontside ollie at Steppe Side.

running. They piled materials such as stones, broke
bricks, and dirt into the shapes of ramps and then cov
ered them with rebar and concrete, creating a usabl
skatepark and a hub for the local skate community.

Alv and his friends showed the world that anyon
could make a skatepark for relatively low cost, wit
minimal experience, and with or without permission
Steppe Side started a DIY skatepark-building craz
that circled the globe and redefined what a skate
park could be. In reality, do-it-yourself skatepark
are anything but an individual activity. They ar
about friends working and sweating together t
build something that will bring years of enjoymen
to an entire community.

For a long time, DIY parks were rare outliers. Bu
Alv's crew showed the world that anyone could d
it if they just started small and kept at it. Municipal
ities occasionally demolish these structures, bu
many parks go unnoticed for years at a time. Stepp
Side has been demolished twice, and both time
skaters have rebuilt it. When you step inside a DIY
park, you feel empowered, like you are part of an
elite secret society in which only you and the othe
skaters understand the rules.

CHAPTER 3

AFRICA

YOUTHS DIRT RIDE NEAR MORONDAVA, MADAGASCAR.

"WHILE THE SUN IS RISING ON THE AVENUE OF THE BAOBABS, THE LOCAL KIDS TAKE TURNS PUSHING DOWN THE DIRT ROAD."

—PATRIK WALLNER, PHOTOGRAPHER

Skateboarding is relatively new in many countries in Africa. So when I heard rumors of a marble paradise in the middle of Morocco, I had my doubts. Nevertheless, I had to find out for myself. I invited a couple of pro-skater friends to come check out the local scene with me.

A city made of marble Agadir was not. But local skaters Ali, Mohamed, and Rachid immediately befriended us, showing us their favorite skate spots. Most of the city was rough for skating, but there was one marble plaza near the beach that had a perfect ledge going off a set of stairs. This became our go-to location each day. Maybe this was the legendary land of marble that we had heard about.

Ali insisted that our large group of foreign and local skateboarders have dinner with him in an Agadir suburb. We followed our host down a quiet, dimly lit street lined with stucco houses with small windows, up a narrow staircase, and into his warm, modest home. As is customary in Morocco, we all gathered around on a long couch that wrapped around a circular table, upon which our hosts placed a massive platter of lamb and couscous. We each dug into the shared platter with our own spoon. It was a new experience to negotiate a particular triangle of couscous with my nearest neighbor. It made me appreciate how tightly knit the Agadir skate community is, in a way that is perhaps rare in the United States. I've seen the same spirit of communalism in other parts of Africa, including in Ethiopia, where we were invited into a local skater's home for the slaughtering of a goat—a rare occasion held in our honor.

The common experience of skateboarding can connect us to people in cultures so different from our own. This holds true in a neighborhood in Brooklyn, New York, just as it does in Morocco or Ethiopia. And this connection has the power to improve people's lives in many places throughout Africa and around the world.

The most established skate scene on the continent is in South Africa, which is frequently visited by professional skateboarders from Europe and the United States. The nonprofit organization Skateistan recently opened a skateboarding school in Johannesburg, extending its mission of helping underprivileged children and young adults by promoting equality and education.

In Uganda, one town's skate scene blossomed in 2006 when local entrepreneur Jackson Mubiru and South African student Shael Swart built a skatepark in Kitintale, a neighborhood in Uganda's capital city of Kampala. Mubiru later founded the Uganda Skateboard Union, which sponsors local youths and provides them with greater opportunities through skateboarding and education. The Union also hosts contests and invites skaters from the neighboring countries of Kenya and Tanzania, where skateparks have recently been built, to participate.

In my experience, skateboarders are communal creatures, in Africa and around the world. They stick together and look out for one another. And perhaps there is no greater need for that than in Africa, where the resources are so scarce and the problems so vast. ∎

JOSEPH BIAIS ~ MERZOUGA, MOROCCO
Trick: 5050 grind

"IT'S COMMON TO COME ACROSS SUCH FRIENDLINESS ON THE STREETS; PEOPLE CLEARING THE WAY AND HOLDING TRAFFIC."

—AARON "JAWS" HOMOKI

AARON "JAWS" HOMOKI ~ ADDIS ABABA, ETHIOPIA
Trick: Kickflip melon grab

KANYA SPANI REALIZES YOU SOMETIMES HAVE TO PAY TO PLAY ~ CAPE TOWN, SOUTH AFRICA.
Trick: Bluntslide

NYJAH HUSTON ~ ADDIS ABABA, ETHIOPIA
Trick: Nosegrind

"WHEN SOMEONE AS COLOR COORDINATED AS THIS YOUNG MAN WALKS BY A SPOT, YOU HAVE TO GET THE PHOTO. THIS COULDN'T HAVE WORKED OUT BETTER."

—MATT PRICE, PHOTOGRAPHER

MARTY MURAWSKI ~ BELLVILLE, SOUTH AFRICA
Trick: Noseslide

DERRICK WILSON ~ ADDIS ABABA, ETHIOPIA
Trick: Kickflip

"THE LONG DRIVE TO THIS SPOT WAS WORTH IT WHEN WE MET A HANDFUL OF KIDS WHO HAD NEVER SKATED BEFORE. THE JOY ON THEIR FACES WAS PRICELESS!"

—SAM CLARK, PHOTOGRAPHER

CHILDREN HAVE FUN WITH A SKATEBOARD ~
WILLOWMORE, SOUTH AFRICA.

DOUGLAS MWESIGWA ~ KAMPALA, UGANDA
Trick: Ollie

YANN HOROWITZ - SWAKOPMUND, NAMIBIA
Trick: Boneless

MEGABI SKATE
Addis Ababa, Ethiopia

When I arrived at Israel "Izzy" Dejene's house in a van full of pro skaters, the sheer number of kids was overwhelming at first. As the door opened, hundreds of hands came reaching out for us, everyone trying to get our attention. It was then that I began to understand the magnitude of the project that Izzy was leading.

We had come to help Izzy's organization, Megabi Skate, build the first concrete half-pipe in Ethiopia. I knew that Megabi Skate's goal was to help provide creative outlets and support for underprivileged youths. But when I was there on the ground, I realized that without Izzy's leadership, these kids would be lost on the street. Many were orphans who had made their way to Addis Ababa looking for work. Some as young as four had found their way into Izzy's care. Through skateboarding and music, Izzy has created a tight-knit community of young skaters, musicians, and performers that transcends conditions of poverty and low self-esteem.

When Izzy was young, he received the nickname "Megabi," meaning "one who gives life to others." But it wasn't until he saw kids in his rough neighborhood using scraps of plastic on their shoes to slide downhill

(At the Megabi Skate ramp, from top to bottom) Four-year-old "President Dougy" (left) wants to be president in 30 years; Brian Pino from California Skateparks puts the finishing touches on the ramp; Israel "Izzy" Dejene, founder of Megabi Skate.

"SHARING THE LOVE OF SKATEBOARDING WITH KIDS HALFWAY ACROSS THE WORLD HAS BEEN LIFE CHANGING."

—NYJAH HUSTON

Pro skaters pose with the Megabi Skate crew on the Dream Big Stage, where the kids perform talent shows every week.

that he finally realized the significance of his nickname. Izzy had fallen in love with skateboarding several years earlier on a trip to Sweden. He now understood that it would engage the local kids and help increase their confidence, leadership skills, and sense of community. Shortly thereafter, Megabi Skate was born.

The skateboard ramp was already under way when we arrived. Young children volunteered to help out, along with Izzy's family and our group of skaters. Everyone pitched in to shovel gravel and sand, mix concrete, and form the ramp.

Once the ramp was completed, pro skateboarders, including Tony Hawk and Nyjah Huston, performed a demonstration to inspire the kids to keep skating.

As we departed that evening, Izzy left us with these parting words: "It doesn't matter how big or small [the things are that] we do to make a change or give back. Everything we do with love will make a big impact."

Tony Hawk performs a tuck knee invert at an exhibition celebrating the opening

CHAPTER 4

WESTERN

ASIA

DAVE BACHINSKY ~ ALMATY, KAZAKHSTAN
Trick: Frontside kickflip

"FIRSTHAND EXPERIENCE IS THE BEST WAY TO DISCOVER A NEW COUNTRY. SOMETIMES SKATEBOARDING TAKES YOU FURTHER THAN YOU EVER IMAGINED."

—KIRILL KOROBKOV, JOURNALIST

During my many years of shooting for skate magazines, I produced trips to places that no professional skater had gone before. I would literally stare at a world map to find cities I'd never heard of or even thought of traveling to before. I'd research the city online, and if it looked like there was enough infrastructure for skate spots to exist, I'd start planning my trip. One of those cities was Astana, the recently modernized capital of Kazakhstan.

In the fall of 2008, I gathered a group of professional skaters to explore Almaty and Astana, the seemingly unskated cities of the Central Asian country. We didn't expect to find any other skaters on the trip, but within several hours of arriving, we met a young skateboarder named Victor and a few of his friends. Our crew, a mix of skaters from the United States, Europe, and Kazakhstan, appears on pages 148-49, spending a leisurely afternoon at one of the barely skated public spaces in the city.

Astana, with its brand-new construction, turned out to be a gold mine of skate spots. Buildings seemed to pop up out of the flat landscape like an architect's dream. We saw huge pyramids made of metal and glass, and a bizarre tower made of white spines that jutted skyward, holding a massive golden sphere hundreds of feet off the ground. In the plentiful marble plazas surrounding the buildings, skate spots were everywhere. Not only was Astana's architecture perfect for a creative skater, but also the city was nearly a ghost town. It was built for a population that had yet to arrive.

Coming from the States, it was a rare luxury to have relaxed skate sessions without pedestrians wandering into the shot or security guards hassling us. One of the pros, Jack Sabback, could attempt difficult tricks like his nosegrind (pages 152-53) over and over without fear of crashing into anyone. Jack would ollie onto the ledge before the first set of stairs and grind along it while balanced on his front truck, until he passed the second set of stairs and then landed on the ground below—all without touching the nose of his board or his back truck to the ledge.

The funny thing about street skating is that what is a spot to one person may not be a spot to another. A skater's creativity and skill level dictates what is or isn't a spot. So it could be a potentially life-altering event for the few skaters living in Astana to see professional skaters in action. Once you see what's possible, your own skating can flourish rapidly. In person (rather than on the Internet), you see the experts' struggles and triumphs and grasp a real understanding of what goes into a single trick. I hope that we left the locals with a positive impression and a desire to strive for higher levels of difficulty.

My habit of map-gazing soon led me to destinations such as Baku, Azerbaijan; Ankara, Turkey; and the island of Cyprus. Each journey propelled me forward. I realized that I needed to keep going and continue searching for unusual locations and the fascinating people who skate them. ■

WIEGER VAN WAGENINGEN ~ ALMATY, KAZAKHSTAN
Trick: Frontside heelflip

SKATEBOARDERS TRAVELING BY RAIL ~ ASTANA, KAZAKHSTAN

EXHAUSTED, DARYL ANGEL AND DONOVON PISCOPO WAIT FOR A FLIGHT ~ BAKU, AZERBAIJAN.

A GROUP OF EUROPEAN AND IRANIAN SKATEBOARDERS PUSH DOWN A
STREET BENEATH A PORTRAIT OF AYATOLLAH KHOMEINI ~ TEHRAN, IRAN.

"I VISITED THE ZAATARI REFUGEE CAMP, WHERE MANY CHILDREN HAVE NOT LEFT THE CAMP IN YEARS AND ARE UNDERSTIMULATED. SKATEBOARDING IS THE PERFECT OUTLET."

—DANIEL ZVEREFF, PHOTOGRAPHER

AN AID WORKER HELPS A YOUNG GIRL TRY SKATEBOARDING ~ ZAATARI REFUGEE CAMP, JORDAN.

GOSHA KONYSHEV ~ KABUL, AFGHANISTAN
Trick: Kickflip

"FOR A SKATEBOARDER, A GUARD WIELDING A GUN IS A NO-CONTEST SITUATION, BUT WHEN YOU REALIZE HE'S NOT CONCERNED WITH SKATING, YOU ALMOST FEEL LIKE HE'S PROTECTING YOU."

—JAMIE THOMAS

JAMIE THOMAS ~ KABUL, AFGHANISTAN
Trick: Ollie

SKATEBOARDERS WATCH A FRIEND TRY A TRICK ~ ASTANA, KAZAKHSTAN.

DONOVON PISCOPO ~ BAKU, AZERBAIJAN
Trick: Wallride to 5-0 grind

JACK SABBACK ~ ASTANA, KAZAKHSTAN
Trick: Nosegrind

SKATEISTAN
Kabul, Afghanistan

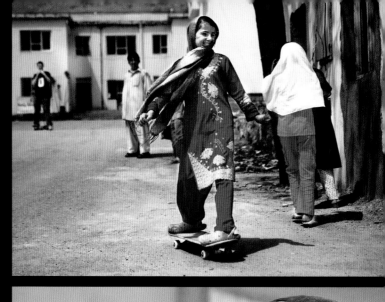

When Oliver Percovich followed his then girlfriend from Australia to Afghanistan in 2006, he wasn't about to leave his skateboard behind. Skating in the streets of Kabul, he quickly became the object of children's fascination. The young Afghan girls and boys were utterly captivated and sometimes actually tried to grab his skateboard so they could take a spin. Percovich soon realized the potential the sport could have for the youths of the war-torn country.

He began to host informal skate sessions at an orphanage outside Kabul, where the kids would skate in an abandoned fountain. On one occasion, a group of girls from different ethnic and economic backgrounds started skating together and soon began to sing and dance and hold hands. Percovich quickly recognized that skateboarding could be a powerful weapon in the fight against cultural and economic prejudices.

The seeds of Skateistan had been planted. After two years of grassroots fundraising and support from the international aid community, Percovich opened the first Skateistan facility in Kabul in 2009. Built on and donated by the Afghan Olympic Committee, it is the first skatepark and largest sports facility in the country. Skateistan promotes community, youth

(Skateistan students, from top to bottom) A young girl skates down a street in Kabul, Afghanistan; two children help each other fasten their helmets at Kabul's Skateistan indoor skatepark; skaters pass by guards in Kabul

"THE KEY IS NOT SKATEBOARDING;
THE KEY IS THE POWER OF SHARING
SOMETHING THAT YOU LOVE."

—OLIVER PERCOVICH

engagement, education, and creativity through skate-boarding and now has 1,000 attendees in Afghanistan alone. Forty percent of the skaters are female, which is perhaps the largest percentage of females at any skate school in the world. Afghan girls, who are restricted from most sports and many jobs, are being allowed to skate unimpeded. Skating simply hasn't been around long enough for anyone to decide it should be prohibited.

In 2013, Skateistan was named by the *Global Journal* as one of the top 100 nongovernmental organizations worldwide, and has since built facilities in Mazar-i-Sharif, Afghanistan, as well as in Cambodia and South Africa. The organization invites all youths to attend and focuses on helping those from disadvantaged backgrounds. It's remarkable to see how a common passion helps kids transcend cultural barriers that have lingered for centuries.

Hanifa Qayumi and Bilal Mir Bat Zai ride a skateboard in the destroyed Darul

CHAPTER 5

EASTERN ASIA

& OCEANIA

SEAN MALTO ~ NEW DELHI, INDIA
Trick: 5050 grind

"**THIS SPOT WAS LITERALLY ABOVE A RIVER OF SEWAGE. IT MADE ME THINK ABOUT WHAT'S IMPORTANT IN LIFE.**"

—SEAN MALTO

Our motorbike engines whirred as we climbed the winding mountain road. Clouds of exhaust engulfed us as buses hurtled along the centerline without regard for lowly motorcyclists traveling in the opposite direction. Spanish pro Javier Mendizabal and I rounded a bend and a village appeared, with small shanties on the side of the road, and then dropped out of view over the hillside. Letting off the gas a little, we entered the cluster of homes and noticed a group of kids playing in the dirt. They had something with them, which became visible only when a plume of dust cleared: skateboards. This was completely astounding. Javier and I were on a skateboarding tour through Vietnam, but we never expected to see other skaters in a rural village in the Central Highlands. We slammed on the brakes and stopped to have a closer look.

The year was 2012, but the boards looked like something from the sixties—long, dusty planks with four metal wheels attached to wooden axles (pages 172-73). The kids ran off at first and hid their boards inside one of the houses. The language barrier was too great for verbal communication, so we let our skateboards do the talking. We unpacked our boards and started skating in the road in front of them, taking care to dodge the buses that flew by every few minutes.

The children were magnetically drawn to our boards. They realized that we shared something in common. Soon, one of the kids ran to get his homemade board, and we began laughing and trying out each other's wheels. The kids' parents and neighbors came out to watch as

Javier, the local kids, and I all skated in the street, showing each other our tricks and techniques. The kids had never seen modern skateboards before and were totally enchanted. They kept laughing and falling because the wheels on our boards rolled so fast.

When I look back at the photos, I can see that everyone was smiling at the scene unfolding in front of them. I wish we could have stayed longer and spoken with the parents about how they made the boards and where they got the designs. Both Javier and I wanted to leave something behind, so he gave them an extra board and I left my cruiser (a skateboard with large soft wheels), which would help the kids skate on the bumpy terrain. On our long journey through Vietnam, these were the only skaters we met outside of Hanoi and Saigon. I can only wonder if they are still skating and building ramps, or if the boards we left behind have been thrown away, lost down the mountain, or used for a more practical purpose. One day I hope to return and find out.

In Asian cities such as Bangkok, Shanghai, and Tokyo, skateboarding has become its own industry. There, as in the United States, Australia, and Europe, top pros skate the best spots and use the best urban infrastructure. But seeing those kids in rural Vietnam brought the sport back to basics. It was a window into the magic of skateboarding and the thrill it inspires at first sight. In a small way, it reminded me of my beginnings in skating, of building a ramp with plywood scraps and piles of firewood—and of using what we had to make our own fun. ▪

MICHAEL MACKRODT ~ DONG HOI, VIETNAM
Trick: Frontside blunt

PHILLIP MARSHALL ~ ADELAIDE, AUSTRALIA
Trick: Backside noseblunt

"A HUGE PART OF SKATEBOARDING BOTH PHYSICALLY AND CULTURALLY IS DISCOVERING THINGS YOU DIDN'T KNOW YOU WERE LOOKING FOR."

—JACK SABBACK

JACK SABBACK ~ ULAANBAATAR, MONGOLIA
Trick: Backside lipslide

A MOTORBIKE PACKED WITH A SKATEBOARD ~ NEAR HÒA BÌNH, VIETNAM

DILAPIDATED SKATE SHOES ~ DEO HAI VAN, VIETNAM

CHILDREN SHOW OFF THEIR HOMEMADE SKATEBOARD ~
CENTRAL HIGHLANDS, VIETNAM.

"WAKING UP EARLY IS A MUST, ESPECIALLY WHEN SKATING SPOTS ARE IN THE CENTER OF THE CITY, WHERE MY BOARD HAS THE POSSI- BILITY OF FALLING ON PEOPLE'S HEADS."

—KENNY REED

KENNY REED ~ HONG KONG, CHINA
Trick: Kickflip

PAUL BATTLAY ~ ORDOS, CHINA
Trick: Boneless

DAN PLUNKETT ~ TOKYO, JAPAN
Trick: Noseslide transfer

"SKATEBOARDING DESTROYS ALL BARRIERS. IT ENABLES YOU TO CONNECT WITH EVERYTHING, NO MATTER WHAT LANGUAGE YOU SPEAK, WHERE YOU LIVE, OR HOW DIFFERENT YOU ARE."

—BEN GORE

BEN GORE ~ TOKYO, JAPAN
Trick: Wallie

LOCAL SKATER NANAE FUJIWARA ~ OSAKA, JAPAN

KEVIN TERPENING TAKES A BREAK ~ SEOUL, SOUTH KOREA.

"WE LOST TONS OF BOARDS INTO THE OCEAN THAT DAY. IT WAS OUR SACRIFICE TO THE SKATE GODS!"

—OMAR HASSAN

OMAR HASSAN ~ SYDNEY, AUSTRALIA
Trick: Backside air

JOEY PEPPER ~ KEELUNG, TAIWAN
Trick: Blunt to fakie

SEOUL, SOUTH KOREA

OSAKA, JAPAN

"SKATEBOARDING IS MAGICAL. WHAT ELSE IS THERE TO SAY?"

—JONATHAN MEHRING

CHILDREN CELEBRATE SKATEBOARDING ~ JAIPUR, INDIA.

CHRISTIAN LOW ~ ORDOS, CHINA
Trick: Wallride

HOLYSTOKED
Bangalore, India

In 2013, an Indian skate collective called Holystoked partnered with Levi's Skateboarding and German skatepark creators 2er Builders to construct the first free skatepark in India. The goal was to design an easily rideable and creatively built park that would engage skaters of different skill levels.

A crew of skaters, builders, and volunteers from Europe, India, and the United States arrived in the city of Bangalore to clear a plot of land and build a professionally made park in less than two weeks. Local children gathered around each day to watch the progress. The kids could hardly stand the wait, so one of the builders cut a piece of scrap wood into an oblong shape and bolted an old set of trucks and wheels to it. It soon became the locally shared skateboard, with kids pushing one another up and down the street next to the park. They took one tumble after another, knocking one another off the board and trying to ride two at a time. Their tricks always ended in disaster, but that didn't deter future attempts. They were ravenous for more.

Skaters are the only ones who truly understand how a skatepark can transform a community, providing a place for underprivileged kids to channel their energies

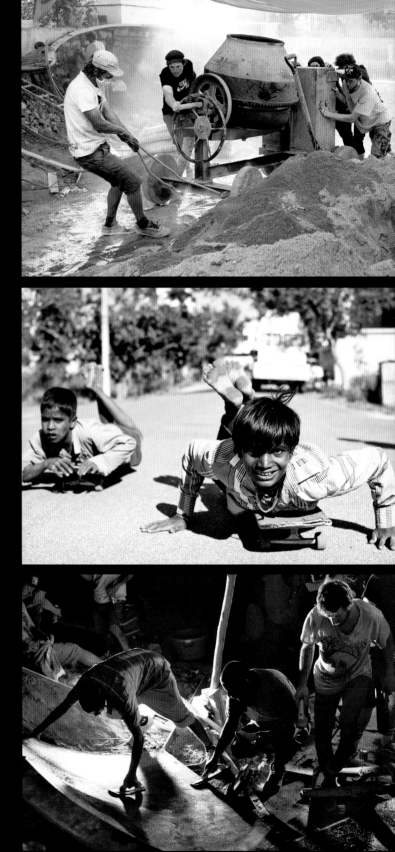

(During construction of the Holystoked skatepark, from top to bottom) Members of the 2er Builders crew help move a cement mixer; neighborhood children discover skateboarding with boards lent out by the builders; skaters smoothing the surface of a concrete ramp.

**"THE PARK BUILD
WAS PRETTY MUCH THE HIGHLIGHT OF THEIR LIVES
FOR MANY OF THE SKATERS AND THE KIDS IN BANGALORE."**

—ABHISHEK ENBAKE

Daryl Nobbs pulls off a stalefish at the opening of Holystoked park.

and to be part of something bigger than themselves. This was the gift that the volunteers wanted to give to this community.

After a few mishaps, broken tools, miscalculated materials, and other minor setbacks, the builders met the two-week deadline. The opening ceremony was a spectacle, with bands playing and pro skaters putting on an exhibition that blew everyone's minds.

The park was a huge success for a time. But in direct opposition to the values on which the park was built, the neighboring property owner had the park shut down just before this book went to press. One of his reasons? Lower-class children were using the park on a daily basis. We can only hope that the closure is temporary. The good news is that the kids helped to build the first park, so now they have the skills to build another one somewhere else.

In the meantime, Holystoked continues to operate in an increasing number of locations in India, promoting skateboarding and teaching youths the skills to make their own skate spots. The revolution has just begun!

Holystoked founders Abhishek Enbake and Shashank "Soms" Somanna skate down a street in Bangalore, India.

CHAPTER 6

SOUTH

BRIAN DELATORRE ~ MEDELLÍN, COLOMBIA
Trick: Kickflip

"IN PLACES WHERE SKATING IS NEW, THE LOCALS ARE MORE INTRIGUED THAN IRRITATED."

—BRIAN DELATORRE

Batman ran up the facade of a steep embankment. It was an artfully designed building, part of a larger urban sculpture in Belém, Brazil. He ascended the top, skateboard in hand, and without hesitation fitted the tail on top in the position to drop in. Our crew heard his battle cry as he committed. Batman leaned forward, putting four wheels down on the slanted wall as the ground rushed toward him. He pulled up to land centered on the ground below, but it was too late. He pummeled the pavement with his body and barely managed to tumble out of disaster. He jumped up enthusiastically and ran back up the embankment. As he leaned forward to try again, a couple of armed guards started shouting at him to stop. This time he leveled out too early for impact, falling once again. We cheered, knowing that the next attempt was sure to be a make, but the guards weren't having it. We politely excused ourselves and went along our way. Under his breath, Batman vowed to return and conquer the steep bank once and for all.

Joelcio "Batman" Araujo and Augusto Formiga, two local skaters, hosted my group at this stop on a riverboat trip up the Amazon. I'd organized a crew of Brazilian and American pros to join me on the journey and to skate the main urban centers along the way (pages 206-207, 222-23, and 227).

As Batman proved, there is something about skating in South America that makes skaters fearless. It has to do with the rough pavement and aging infrastructure typical of the continent's cities. To become a skilled skateboarder in this environment, you have to be tough, because if you fall, you will pay for it. Skaters from South America are inherently good at skating, falling, and adapting to new terrain. Professional skater and 12-time X Games champion Bob Burnquist made waves in the skate community in 2001 when he became the first skater to ride a full loop ramp "switch stance"—the equivalent of a right-footer riding left-footed. He grew up skating the rugged concrete and metal ramps of São Paulo, Brazil, and is considered one of the most influential ramp skaters, next to Danny Way and Tony Hawk.

David Gonzalez, originally from Medellín, Colombia, was awarded *Thrasher Magazine*'s Skater of the Year in 2012 after starring in an online video titled "Possessed to Skate." The stunt he performed pushed the boundaries of what was considered physically possible on a skateboard.

While Colombia, Peru, Chile, Argentina, and Bolivia all have burgeoning skate scenes, Brazil is South America's skateboarding hot spot. Every year Brazilian skaters make waves in the industry, and many relocate to California and become well-known professional skaters. São Paulo native Rodrigo Teixeira (pages 208-209) has been a staple of the U.S. skating scene for more than a decade, with his signature "tech-gnar" (technical and gnarly—i.e., dangerous) combination of tricks. Every year younger blood keeps showing up to blow minds. The determined innovators of South America have pushed skateboarding to higher levels around the world, leaving their permanent mark on the sport's history for all to see. ▪

MEHRING'S CREW OF PROS DISEMBARK FROM A RIVERBOAT IN THE AMAZON ~ SANTARÉM, BRAZIL.

RODRIGO TEIXEIRA ~ SÃO PAULO, BRAZIL
Trick: Frontside half-cab kickflip

"SOMETIMES IT FEELS LIKE EVERYTHING IS AGAINST YOU. HIGH ALTITUDE, DUST, AND ROUGH GROUND MADE DYLAN BATTLE THIS SPOT FOR MORE THAN TWO HOURS."

—JONATHAN MEHRING

DYLAN RIEDER ~ LA PAZ, BOLIVIA
Trick: Backside kickflip

LOCAL SKATERS ~ EL ALTO, BOLIVIA

CHILDREN SHARE A SKATEBOARD ~ LA PAZ, BOLIVIA.

FRED GALL ~ LA PAZ, BOLIVIA
Trick: Ollie attempt

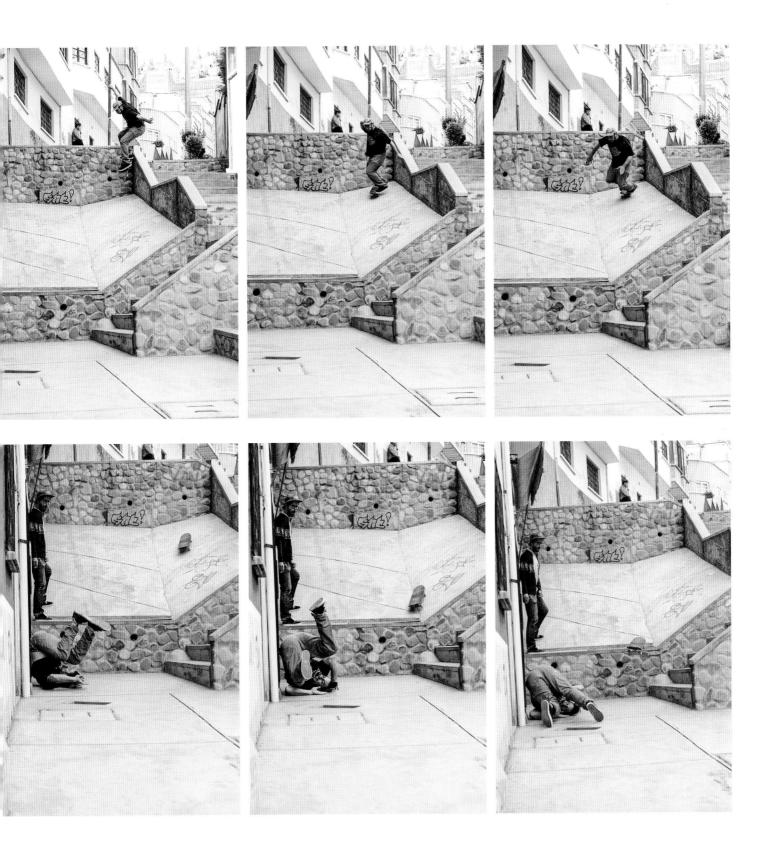

BOBBY WORREST - LA PAZ, B
Trick: Frontside

"THE MOMENT OF TRUTH: DROPPING IN. THIS IS ONE OF THE MOST BASIC AND YET, FOR BEGINNERS, MOST FRIGHTENING MANEUVERS."

—JONATHAN MEHRING

A YOUTH TAKES HIS FIRST "DROP IN" ~ MEDELLÍN, COLOMBIA.

JERRY HSU ~ BUENOS AIRES, ARGENTINA
Trick: Backside smith grind

VAN WASTELL ~ BUENOS AIRES, ARGENTINA
Trick: Backside heelflip

JAKE JOHNSON ~ MANAUS, BRAZIL
Trick: Switch kickflip

"I WAS ON THE VERGE OF PASSING OUT BECAUSE OF THIN AIR—THIS WAS A STRUGGLE."

—BOBBY WORREST

BOBBY WORREST ~ LA PAZ, BOLIVIA
Trick: Feeble grind transfer

NESTOR JUDKINS ~ EL ALTO, BOLIVIA
Trick: Fronside kickflip

KENNY ANDERSON ~ BELÉM, BRAZIL
Trick: Frontside wallride

LUAN OLIVEIRA ~ CRICIÚMA, BRAZIL
Trick: Frontside flip

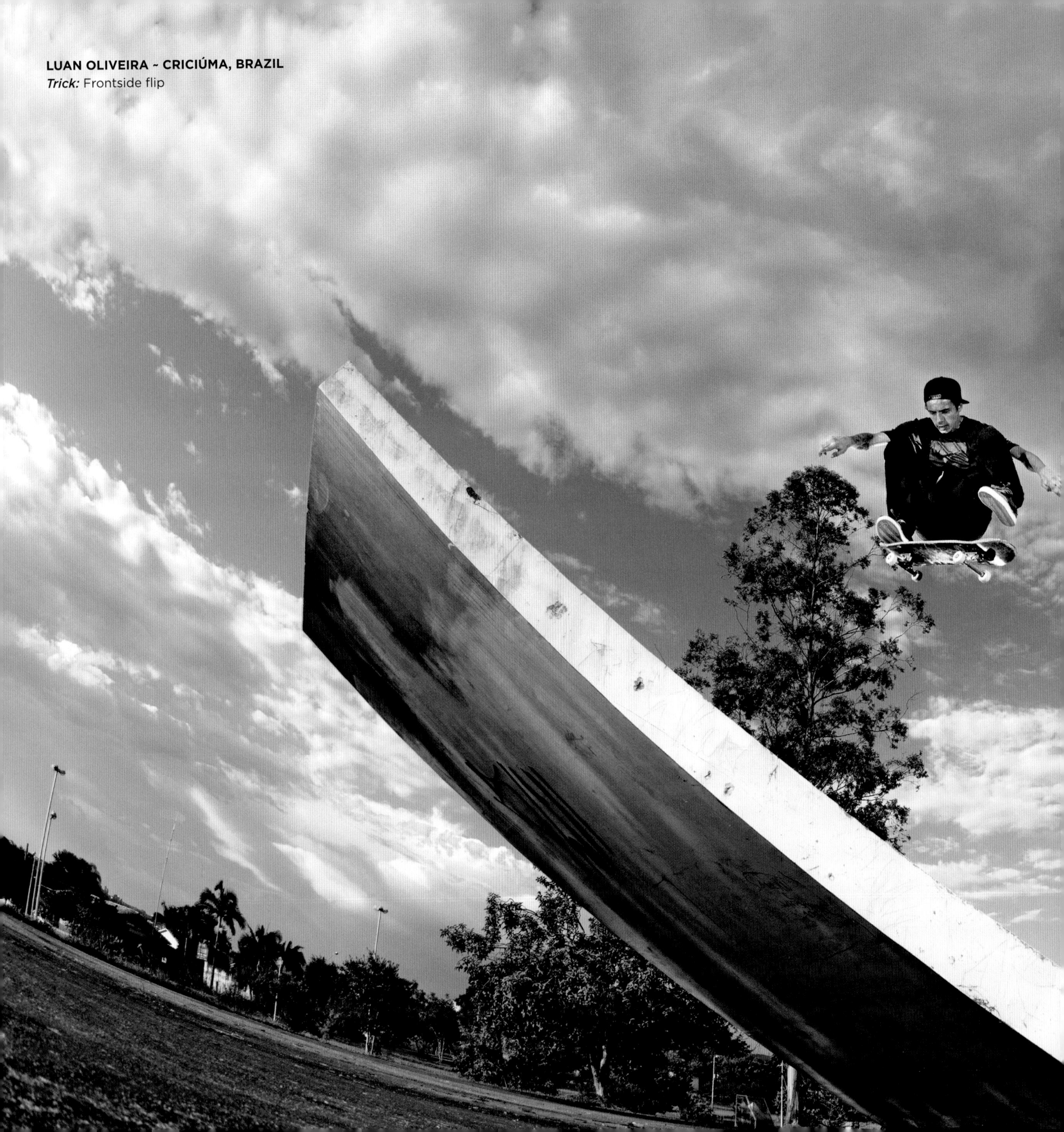

PURA PURA
La Paz, Bolivia

The air in La Paz is thin. At some 12,000 feet, it's a struggle to just walk uphill. Now imagine building a skatepark at this altitude! With the help of lots of coca tea to combat altitude sickness, that's exactly what we did at Parque de Pura Pura.

The nongovernmental organization Make Life Skate Life works closely with Levi's Skateboarding to build sustainable skateparks in cities that need positive activities for young people. In 2013, Make Life Skate Life set its sights on La Paz. A one-month timetable was set to construct a 21,000-square-foot concrete playground for skaters. The project drew 100 volunteers from more than 20 countries who wanted to help build one of the largest skateparks in South America.

Constructing it was tough but satisfying work. Digging out banks and transitions, cutting and tying rebar, fitting templates to shape ramps, mixing and pouring concrete—the process was largely organic, with minimal planning. Saws buzzed, cement mixers rumbled constantly, and above the din, people shouted out directions in multiple languages. Each country's crew would start on its own creation in a corner of the park. The Germans would measure everything, cutting templates to the exact centimeter. The Americans would

(Building Pura Pura, from top to bottom) Builders take a break in the midday heat; skateboarder Jerry Mraz shows off his waterlogged hands; volunteers mix concrete for ramps.

"IT WAS AS IF 100-PLUS ANGELS APPEARED
FROM HEAVEN AND HELL TO MIRACULOUSLY THROW
A BEAUTIFUL SKATEPARK TOGETHER IN A FEW WEEKS."

—MILTON ARELLANO, BOLIVIAN SKATEBOARDER

Skaters test out the first cured-concrete obstacles, as construction of Pura Pura nears completion.

measure their templates and then say, "Forget it," and eyeball the ramp's transition. The Japanese made curving, snakelike bumps and banks. The British and Danish crews constructed huge obstacles that became some of the main ramps in the park. The Spanish-speaking crews built banks, walls, steps, and a crazy concrete volcano with a tree coming out of it. Eventually, one section melded into another. A drainage ditch even became an obstacle with gaps and launch ramps going over it.

Each day more volunteers arrived. As the crowd grew, the park turned into a campsite dotted with tents and fire pits between thatched-roof huts. In this small, temporary village, a sense of community transcended all social and language barriers. People helped each other and learned from one another. There's something about a group of people coming together for a common cause, pushing themselves for a month of heavy manual labor, living in close quarters, and eating meals together that really brings out the good vibes. The park is there. It's amazing. And the locals are waiting for you to come shred it with them.

Pro skater Mathias Hall Laursen performs a frontside alley-oop lien, one of the first tricks performed in the new park.

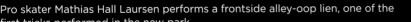

GLOSSARY OF SKATE TERMS

Backside A trick performed when a skater approaches an obstacle with his or her back facing it.

Backside air An air done backside when the skater's front hand grabs the heel edge of the board.

Backside kickflip A kickflip during which the skater and board do a backside 180-degree rotation.

Backside heelflip Same as a backside kickflip but with a heelflip instead of a kickflip.

Backslide lipslide A boardslide performed while approaching backside in which the rear wheels rotate over an obstacle first to create a sliding position.

Bluntslide Sliding the rear wheels of the board along an obstacle while the tail dips below the edge, holding the skater in position.

Boardslide Sliding the middle of the board on an obstacle.

Boneless Placing the front foot on the ground or ramp coping while grabbing the edge of the board with one hand and keeping the back foot on the board.

Crooked grind A nosegrind in which the truck is grinding diagonally on the edge and the nose is sliding on top of an obstacle.

Cruiser A skateboard with large soft wheels.

Deck (or board) The wooden part of a skateboard that you stand on.

Doubles When two people skate the same obstacle at the same time.

Drop in Placing the tail of the board on a coping or on top of an obstacle and leaning forward to begin motion.

Fakie A trick done when the skater approaches an obstacle while rolling in reverse and pops a trick off the tail of the skateboard.

Feeble grind When the back truck is grinding and the front of the board dips over an obstacle.

5050 grind Grinding both the front and the back trucks on an obstacle.

5-0 grind Grinding the back truck on an obstacle while the front is in the air.

Frontside A trick performed when a skater approaches an obstacle with his or her front facing it.

Frontside air An air done frontside while the skater's back hand grabs the toe edge of the board.

Frontside alley-oop An air done frontside while traveling in a backside direction.

Frontside blunt When a skater stalls the rear wheels of the board on top of an obstacle so that the tail dips below the edge, holding the skater in position. Then the skater rotates out of the trick in a frontside direction.

Frontside kickflip A kickflip during which the skater and board do a frontside 180-degree rotation.

Frontside half-cab flip A frontside kickflip performed while approaching the obstacle fakie.

Frontside heelflip Same as a frontside kickflip, but with a heelflip instead of a kickflip.

Frontside rock 'n' roll A ramp trick performed by placing the front wheels over the coping and then rotating front-side 180 degrees back into the transition.

Grind When a skater slides his or her trucks on an obstacle.

Griptape Sandpaper grit tape that provides traction on top of the deck.

Half-cab heelflip A backside heelflip performed when approaching an obstacle fakie.

Heelflip An ollie done while kicking the front foot diagonally off the toe edge of the board to flip it one full rotation.

Hill bombing Riding down a hill at top speed.

Kickflip An ollie done while kicking the front foot diagonally off the heel edge of the board to flip it one full rotation.

Layback grind When a skater lays back, putting a hand on the coping while the board is grinding in front.

Lien air A frontside air where the front hand grabs the heel edge of the board.

Method air Doing a backside air while grabbing the heel edge of the board and pulling it back so that the bottom of the board faces the sky.

Nollie An ollie done while riding forward and popping off the nose.

Nose The front of a skateboard.

Noseblunt slide When the front wheels of the board slide along an obstacle while the nose dips below the edge, holding the skater in position.

Nosegrind Grinding the front truck on an obstacle.

Noseslide Sliding the nose on an obstacle.

Ollie A basic maneuver in which a skater jumps and pops up with the board stuck to his or her feet.

Ollie one-foot (or ollie north) An ollie performed while kicking the front foot forward off the board.

180 When a skater turns 180 degrees during a trick.

Skitching Skating while holding on to a moving vehicle.

Slam A hard fall.

Smith grind When the back truck is grinding and the front of the board dips below the obstacle so that one edge is sliding as well.

Stalefish An ollie or frontside air done when the skater grabs the heel edge of the board between the feet with the back hand.

Switch flip A kickflip performed while approaching the obstacle switch stance.

Switch stance (or switch) Skating with the opposite foot forward (similar to writing with your nondominant hand).

Tail The back of a skateboard.

Tail stall When a skater stops momentarily on top of an obstacle while balanced on the tail of the board.

Tailslide Sliding the tail on an obstacle.

360 flip A kickflip with a 360-degree spin added so that the board flips one full rotation and spins one full rotation simultaneously.

Tic tac When a skater picks up the front wheels of a skateboard by putting pressure on the tail of the board and moving left, right, left, right with his or her front foot, creating forward momentum.

Transfer Landing a trick on the opposite side of the obstacle from where it started.

Truck The metal part of a skateboard that holds the wheels to the deck and allows for turning.

Wallie A combination of an ollie and a wallride, with the skater smacking the wheels on an obstacle while jumping over it.

Wallride Riding all four wheels of the board on a wall or similar vertical surface.

ABOUT THE AUTHOR

JONATHAN MEHRING An award-winning photographer, Mehring has been named one of the most influential people in skateboarding by ESPN and the X Games. Born and raised in central Virginia, and now based in Brooklyn, Mehring has organized groups of pro skaters to travel to every inhabited continent. He has photographed pros and locals in 30 countries, including far-flung places such as Mongolia, the Amazon, and the Australian outback. Mehring's work has been featured in *Rolling Stone* and the *Wall Street Journal* as well as in top skateboarding magazines such as *Thrasher Magazine, Transworld SKATEboarding,* and the *Skateboard Mag.* In 2013, Mehring began partnering with Levi's Skateboarding in their efforts to build skateparks in underserved communities around the world.

ABOUT THE CONTRIBUTORS

TONY HAWK Now the most recognized action sports figure in the world, Tony Hawk was nine years old when his brother changed his life by giving him a blue fiberglass Bahne skateboard. By fourteen he'd turned pro, and by sixteen he was widely considered the best skateboarder on Earth. In 1999, he became the first skater ever to complete a 900, and shortly thereafter, he teamed up with Activision to launch *Tony Hawk's Pro Skater,* now a billion-dollar video game franchise. He has created a Tony Hawk brand that includes Birdhouse Skateboards, Hawk Clothing, and the Tony Hawk Signature Series of sporting goods and toys; authored a *New York Times* best seller; and his 900 Films production company launched the RIDE Channel. His Tony Hawk Foundation has given away more than $5.3 million to 560 skatepark projects throughout the United States.

Contributing Photographers

Loic Benoit Born in Lyon, France, Benoit is a self-taught photographer who specializes in skateboarding and travel imagery. His clients include *Sugar* magazine and Red Bull.

Mike Blabac DC Shoes photographer Blabac has shot some of the most important moments in skateboard history, including pro skater Danny Way's record-setting highest air and Great Wall of China jumps.

Joe Brook A photographer and a former photo editor, Brook is an artistic workhorse and longtime staffer at top skateboarding publication *Thrasher Magazine.*

Michael Burnett An editor and photographer for *Thrasher Magazine* for many years, Burnett's photography has been instrumental in taking the magazine to the top of the industry.

Dave Chami A longtime photographer for *Transworld SKATEboarding* magazine, Chami originally hails from New Zealand and is now based in San Francisco, California.

Sam Clark Specializing in the South African skate scene, Clark's photography provides a unique perspective on skating in his home country. His clients include *Sessions, Thrasher,* and *Kingpin* magazines.

Jake Darwen A senior photographer at Australia's *Slam Skateboarding* magazine, Darwen's work brings a fresh view to skateboard photography that never ceases to inspire and amaze.

Chad Foreman A three-time Lucie Award winner, Foreman specializes in action and landscape imagery. Clients include *Transworld SKATEboarding* magazine, *Thrasher Magazine,* and the *Skateboard Mag.*

Yann Gross Gross's work focuses on identities, issues, and collaborations with communities. His clients include *Aperture, Colors, Frieze,* and the *New York Times Magazine.*

Alex Irvine A former editor of *Kingpin* magazine, Irvine now owns a consulting business and continues to shoot photos around the globe.

Atiba Jefferson A fixture in the Los Angeles skateboard scene for many years, Jefferson is a photo associate at the *Skateboard Mag* and is also a well-known basketball photographer. His clients include ESPN, Nike, and Panasonic.

Alexey Lapin Originally from Kazakhstan, Lapin now resides in Moscow and has been photographing skateboarding in Eastern Europe for more than ten years.

Mike O'Meally Australian-born O'Meally is an international photographer based in Los Angeles. Best known for his skateboarding work, his photographic interests span culture, travel, and the human race.

Andrew Peters Peters spends most of his time between Sydney, Los Angeles, and New York. Clients include *Monster Children, Desillusion, Skateboarder's Journal,* and Volcom.

Matt Price Originally from Phoenix, Arizona, Price has spent the past nine years traveling and working as a senior photographer for the *Skateboard Mag.*

Jake Simkin Simkin left commercial photography to work in Indonesia after the 2004 tsunami. He has since settled in Afghanistan, where he photographs for the United Nations, nonprofit organizations, and the media.

Nils Svensson Swedish photographer Svensson has documented the skate scene in Malmö since the mid-1990s and currently works for local companies Bryggeriet Skate Org and Polar Skate Co.

Pablo Vaz An action photography specialist, Vaz is based in Brazil and shoots skateboarding and other extreme sports.

Patrik Wallner Wallner is based in Thailand and is constantly on the road self-producing videos, documentaries, and photos about skateboarding.

Daniel Zvereff A New York–based photographer and designer, Zvereff travels to the far corners of the world documenting his journeys through images and journals.

ACKNOWLEDGMENTS

A heartfelt and very special thanks to Susan Tyler Hitchcock for seeing this book's potential and remaining steadfast and determined to see it happen for more than five years.

My utmost gratitude and appreciation goes to Erik Wolsky and Levi's. Without their support, this book would not have been possible. An immense thank you to the National Geographic Books team— Sanaa Akkach, Robin Terry Brown, Adrian Coakley, and Bill O'Donnell—for helping me through the process of making my first book. My deepest appreciation goes to Tony Hawk for contributing the foreword to this book. Thank you to the magazine editors who gave me a chance when I was starting out: Joe Brook, Mark Whiteley, Ted Newsome, and especially Jaime Owens for supporting my travels and helping me realize my vision. I'm ever grateful to the skaters who appear in these pages and who stuck with me through our travels and to the photographers, editors, team managers, videographers, and skateboard companies who helped in the culmination of this project. And thanks to all the local skaters we met along the way, who helped us with translation, meals, locations, and keeping things running smoothly. I am grateful to Thomas Daniel for being a mentor, for pushing me to be a better photographer, and for giving me encouragement to find my vision. And thanks to James Lee for introducing me to skateboarding.

From my heart, a special thanks to my mother and father for always supporting me and allowing me to follow my dreams.

And most of all, a loving thank you to my beautiful wife, Heather, for her enduring support, for being there when I'm on the road, for being so understanding, and for helping me be a better person.

ILLUSTRATIONS CREDITS

All photographs by Jonathan Mehring unless otherwise noted below.

12-13, Chad Foreman; 16, Joe Brook; 32, Mike Blabac; 33, Mike Blabac; 34-35, Andrew Peters; 38-39, Michael Burnett; 40, Michael Burnett; 48-49, Atiba Jefferson; 56-57, Mike Blabac; 64, Dave Chami; 74, Joe Brook; 92-93, Alexey Lapin; 96-97, Joe Brook; 98 (ALL), Nils Svensson; 99, Nils Svensson; 100-101, Nils Svensson; 104, Patrik Wallner; 108-109, Loïc Benoit; 112-113 (ALL), Sam Clark; 116-117, Matt Price; 120-121, Sam Clark; 122-123, Yann Gross; 124-125, Sam Clark; 132, Alexey Lapin; 140-141, Patrik Wallner; 142, Daniel Zvereff; 144-145 (BOTH), Alexey Lapin; 146-147, Chad Foreman; 154 (UP), Skateistan; 154 (CT), Chad Foreman; 154 (LO), Chad Foreman; 155, Jake Simkin; 156-157, Chad Foreman; 166-167, Jake Darwen; 176-177, Jake Darwen; 180-181, Dave Chami; 186-187, Mike O'Meally; 194-195, Jake Darwen; 197, Alex Irvine; 208-209, Dave Chami; 228-229, Pablo Vaz.

Author photo, Mike Manzoori